Supercharged *means great recipes that charge you up, make you feel good and keep you healthy. It is a fresh approach to baking with less refined sugar, different types of flours and alternative techniques. It will help you master the art of baking the healthy way. This recipe collection marks the first of many to tackle new areas of baking and will help you gain confidence.*

contents

introduction

—three ways to a healthy baking routine

Baking really doesn't have to be bad for you. There is no reason why you can't have a slice of key lime pie and also feel very good about yourself. All you need are some simple tricks to switch your baking routine to a healthier one. I am not a healthy baker and I love sugar but I believe there is a need for a bit of balance and with a few shortcuts you can easily get to that point as well.

Flours

Flour is an essential ingredient in baking and if you are feeling bloated after eating cake, bread or cookies, it is time to adapt to a new flour habit. Why not try to make one simple change first to get used to alternatives by switching to wholemeal flour. You can make your own wholemeal flour by taking whole wheat grains and milling them. Use it to easily adapt your existing cake recipes or try spelt flour instead. You can even try adding a bit of rye flour for a higher fibre content. I've done something like that for the Spiced Carrot Cake in this book (pictured opposite). Almond flour is a great gluten free alternative and makes a chocolate cake so much tastier – check out the Flourless Beetroot Chocolate Tart in the 'something sweet' chapter. Polenta can give your bake a lovely Italian flavour. I would recommend starting by substituting half the flours in your recipe with the above alternatives and see how you go. Make sure to add an extra teaspoon of baking powder to increase fluffiness in cakes, though.

Sugars

If you are going to go down the healthy baking route or just want to improve your physical health, cutting down on refined sugars should be right at the top of your list. I have stopped using refined cane sugars and must say I do feel a lot better, and you cannot notice a difference between golden caster sugar and refined sugar in baking although the former has a lot more flavour. I would recommend replacing all refined sugar with raw cane sugar straight away and if a recipe calls for caster sugar, mill your raw sugar for **5 Sec. / Speed 10**. Agave nectar, maple syrup and rice malt syrup are great alternatives to sugar and do not get absorbed by the bloodstream as quickly, preventing a spike in insulin levels. You will notice that in many of the recipes in this collection I have used maple syrup and mentioned the other options so you can decide which one you prefer. A great recipe to utilise maple syrup is my Healthy Lemon Tart which can also be prepared as lemon bars. Rice malt syrup is probably the healthiest choice out of the lot.

Fats

Butter often seems like the only option for baking. This might be true for puff pastry but there is a wide array of ingredients that I have utilised in this recipe collection to make it easier on your waistband and cholesterol levels. For example, extra virgin olive oil is a superb alternative to butter in cake-making, especially for carrot cakes. I often use banana as a replacement for fat, and avocado also works very successfully. Banana is naturally sweet so you can even cut down on any additional sweetener. Avocado is perfect to create texture, for example in ice creams or pies.

starting your day

pumpernickel jars

—tasty with smoked salmon

Pumpernickel is a really dark and wholesome bread and traditionally German. It is prepared by baking on a low temperature in a preserving jar to create a steamy atmosphere and prevent it from drying out. The taste is wonderfully sweet and pumpernickel is the perfect shape for small sandwiches. Top it with some smoked salmon and cucumber slices or make it a kids' lunch sandwich with some cheese and ham and you have yourself a long-lasting meal full of fibre.

250g rye grains
250g spelt grains
500g milk
2 Tbsp white wine vinegar
150g molasses or black treacle
1 Tbsp dry active yeast (or 30g fresh yeast)
100g spelt flour

50g sunflower seeds
50g linseed or flaxseed
1 Tbsp diastatic malt powder (optional)
1 Tbsp sea salt flakes

20g soft butter (or vegetable spread)
30g oats

1. Place the rye grains in the mixing bowl and mill **20 Sec. / Speed 10**. Transfer to a large bowl and set aside.
2. Place the spelt grains in the mixing bowl and mill **20 Sec. / Speed 10**. Add to the bowl with the rye grains.
3. Pour the milk and the white wine vinegar in the mixing bowl then combine **10 Sec. / Speed 2.5**. Leave to curdle for 10 minutes.
4. Add the molasses and dry active yeast then warm **2 Min./ 37°C / Speed 2.5**. Add the milled grains, spelt flour, sunflower seeds, linseed, diastatic malt powder and sea salt flakes then knead **2 Min. / Kneading Function**.
5. Grease three 850ml Weck Jars with butter and dust generously with oats. Divide the mixture between the three jars (they should be halfway full) and cover loosely with the lid. Place in the oven (there is no need to preheat) and bake at 160°C / 140°C Fan / Gas Mark 3 for 3 hours.
6. Once baked, remove from the oven and seal the lids with the rubber and metal clips while still hot if you want to preserve them. You can store the baked pumpernickel in the jars for up to 1 month in a cold spot in the house. Alternatively, you can remove the bread from the jars and place on a cooling rack. Store in a bread bag for up to 1 week once opened.

breakfast muffins

—turmeric, blueberry & apricot

I could not imagine breakfast without these fruity, colourful little muffins. They are packed with delicious ingredients and the best thing is you can whip up the whole batch and freeze them, so that you have muffins ready for the kids and yourself without any further work. The turmeric adds an extra health kick.

100g walnuts
85g gluten free oats + extra for sprinkling
90g buckwheat flour
25g corn starch
1 Tbsp baking powder
150g dried, soft apricots
160g Greek yoghurt
2 bananas

3 large eggs
80g olive oil
1 tsp turmeric (or less if you don't like the taste)
1 pinch sea salt flakes
200g fresh blueberries (or frozen and thawed) + 30g for decoration

1. Preheat the oven to 180°C / 160°C Fan / Gas Mark 4. Line two muffin trays with cupcake liners. If you only have one tray, just leave half the batter in the mixing bowl and cover it with cling film while baking the first batch.
2. Place the walnuts, gluten free oats, buckwheat flour, corn starch and baking powder in the mixing bowl. Blitz 5 Sec. / Speed 10. Transfer to a separate bowl and set aside.
3. Place the apricots, Greek yoghurt and bananas in the mixing bowl. Combine 10 Sec. / Speed 6, then scrape down with spatula. Add the eggs, olive oil, turmeric and sea salt flakes then combine 20 Sec. / Speed 4. Add in the blueberries and mix 15 Sec. / Reverse Speed 3. If the blueberries are not fully incorporated, use your spatula to help.
4. Pour the mixture into the muffin cases, filling them up halfway. Sprinkle with a few oats and top off with some blueberries. Bake in the oven for 20-25 minutes until golden brown and a skewer inserted comes out clean.

coconut buckwheat granola

Breakfast is the most important meal of the day. I am a big fan of granola and always on the lookout for new combinations to try at home. I recently went to my favourite breakfast spot in London, Dishoom, a lovely place for Bombay street food. They served the most amazing spiced Granola. I immediately went home and tried to recreate it. With the added kick of coconut, I have made this tasty version of the original, which is pretty close and delicious served with some Greek yoghurt and fresh fruit.

125g coconut oil
50g maple syrup (or agave nectar or rice malt syrup)
½ tsp vanilla extract
125g water
50g whole almonds
50g whole cashew nuts
50g whole hazelnuts
30g sunflower seeds

10g pumpkin seeds
10g linseed
1 tsp ground cinnamon
½ tsp sea salt flakes
100g buckwheat groats (sometimes called raw buckwheat)
80g buckwheat flour
350g gluten free oats
50g coconut flakes

1. Preheat the oven to 200°C / 180°C Fan / Gas Mark 6. Line a large rectangular baking tray with greaseproof paper.
2. Place the coconut oil, maple syrup, vanilla extract and water in the mixing bowl. Melt 4 Min. / 55°C / Speed 1.
3. Add the whole almonds, whole cashew nuts, whole hazelnuts, sunflower seeds, pumpkin seeds, linseed, ground cinnamon, sea salt flakes, buckwheat groats, buckwheat flour and gluten free oats. Combine 15 Sec. / Reverse / Speed 3. It should be a thick, sticky mass.
4. Transfer the mixture onto the baking tray and spread evenly using a spatula. It should form a single layer but can have clusters here and there.
5. Bake in the oven for 20-25 minutes, stirring every 10 minutes or so. In the last 3 minutes, add the coconut flakes and bake until golden brown while watching the coconut flakes before they brown too quickly.
6. Remove and leave to cool. You can break up the clusters of granola as much as you wish. Store in a large glass jar for up to 1 month.

a whole lotta loaf

Isn't it great when you can memorise only one recipe and make so many different things with it? This wholemeal bread recipe gives you the option to make a large loaf for sandwiches, amazingly fluffy bread rolls for soup or burgers or a pizza base for a great dinner with the family. Although made with wholemeal bread flour, this recipe contains a small percentage of strong white bread flour. If you prefer to use only wholemeal flour, you may wish to add a little water if the dough feels a bit dry.

300g water

1 Tbsp dry active yeast (or 30g fresh yeast)

20g olive oil

10g honey

400g strong wholemeal bread flour

100g strong white bread flour

1 Tbsp sea salt flakes

1. Place the water, dry active yeast, olive oil and honey in the mixing bowl. Warm **2 Min. / 37°C / Speed 2.5.**
2. Add the strong wholemeal bread flour, strong white bread flour and sea salt flakes then knead **2 Min. / Kneading Function.** Transfer into a large glass bowl and cover with cling film. Leave to rise for 1-2 hours at room temperature until doubled in size. Preheat the oven to 200°C / 180°C Fan / Gas Mark 6.

Shaping a loaf

Line a 2-pound loaf tin with greaseproof paper. Transfer the dough onto a lightly floured surface. Flatten and shape it into a rectangle the length of the tin with your fingers. Roll up lengthways and place seam-side down into the prepared tin. Cover with a tea towel and leave to rise for another 45 minutes. Score the top with a knife lengthways. Place in the oven, spray the oven chamber with water and bake for 20-25 minutes until it sounds hollow when tapped.

Preparing a pizza base

Oil two large, round pizza trays with olive oil. Transfer the dough onto a lightly floured surface and divide into two equal pieces. Roll each piece out into a 1.5cm thick circle. Place onto the prepared pizza trays and leave to rest for 10 minutes. Then, prick with a fork all over and use any toppings you like. Brush the crust with oil lightly and bake at 250°C / 230°C Fan / Gas Mark 10 for 15 minutes until golden and crispy.

Making rolls

Transfer the dough onto a lightly floured surface and divide the dough into 6 pieces. Roll each piece into a ball, place on a large rectangular baking tray lined with greaseproof paper and cover with a tea towel. You can sit them quite closely if you want them to touch in the oven. Leave to rise for a further 45 minutes. Place in the oven, spray the oven chamber with water and bake for 12-15 minutes until they sound hollow when tapped.

perfect sandwich toppers

How colourful do these sandwich toppers look? They are not only super healthy and require minimal effort to prepare, you can also store them in the fridge for up to 1 week. You can even store the peanut butter for 2 weeks if it lasts that long. The avocado hummus is perfect as a school or work lunchbox sandwich base. The peanut butter is so smooth and you could use it to make a classic Pb&J sandwich. Or why not try something new and make some avocado spread for breakfast. Add some fresh fruit on top or even a few slices of avocado and you have yourself a healthy start to the day.

Peanut Butter Jelly Time

400g peanuts, peeled
½ tsp sea salt flakes

25g maple syrup (or agave nectar,
  honey or rice malt syrup)
20g soft coconut oil

1. Preheat the oven to 200°C / 180°C Fan / Gas Mark 6.
2. Place the peanuts on a large roasting tray and roast in the oven for 5 minutes. Leave to cool for 10 minutes.
3. Tip the peanuts into the mixing bowl, followed by the sea salt flakes, maple syrup and coconut oil. Blitz **1 Min. / Speed 6**, stopping and scraping down the mixture every 20 seconds.
4. Blitz again **4 Min. / Speed 5**, stopping and scraping down the mixture every 30 seconds. Finally, combine **20 Sec. / Speed 7**. Scrape down the mixture. Insert the butterfly whisk then whisk **1 Min. / Speed 4**. Pour the warm peanut butter into a sterilised jar and cool in the fridge for at least 2 hours before using. Store in the fridge for up to 1 month.

Tip: Don't rinse the bowl straight after. Add 250g almond milk, 1 tsp cocoa powder and 10g maple syrup and blitz **30 Sec. /Speed 10**. It makes an excellent chocolate peanut butter milkshake.

Beetroot Hummus

5g fresh parsley
250g cooked beetroot
1 pinch garlic granules
1 lemon, juice only
1 tsp ground cumin

1 can chickpeas + 50g reserved
  chickpea juice
1 pinch sea salt flakes
90g tahini
20g olive oil

1. Place the parsley in the mixing bowl. Blitz **2 Sec. / Speed 7**. Scrape down using spatula. Add the cooked beetroot, garlic granules, lemon juice, ground cumin, chickpeas, chickpea juice, sea salt flakes, tahini and olive oil then combine **10 Sec. / Speed 10**. Pour into a jar and store in the fridge for up to 1 week.

Avocado Spread

1 avocado, stone removed
½ banana
½ lemon, juice only
30g almond milk

1. Place the avocado, banana, lemon juice and almond milk in the mixing bowl. Combine **10 Sec. / Reverse / Speed 5**. Spread over your toast in the morning and top off with some fresh avocado or just have it as a dip during the day with carrot sticks. It makes a great sandwich base.

feel-good snacks

—*Banana Sesame Cookies*
—*Mixed Spiced Nuts*
—*Chocolate Cookie Sandwiches*
—*Oaty Cookies*
—*Broccoli Quinoa Bites*

banana sesame cookies

These banana sesame cookies are so delicious. They remind me of the super tasty sesame balls I used to get at my favourite Chinese restaurant but are a lot healthier. The cinnamon combined with sesame seeds makes a tasty snack that is perfectly bite-sized and ideal for kids' lunchboxes.

3 ripe bananas, halved
240g ground almonds
80g maple syrup (or agave nectar
   or rice malt syrup)

1 tsp ground cinnamon
150g buckwheat flour
60g sesame seeds

1. Preheat the oven to 170°C / 150°C Fan / Gas Mark 3. Line two large rectangular baking trays with greaseproof paper.
2. Place the ripe bananas, ground almonds, maple syrup, ground cinnamon and buckwheat flour in the mixing bowl. Combine **30 Sec. / Speed 5**.
3. Pour the sesame seeds into a shallow bowl.
4. Take half a tablespoonful of the mixture and roll between your hands into a ball. Coat in the sesame seeds and place on the prepared baking tray. Press down slightly and repeat until the mixture is used up.
5. Bake in the oven for 15 minutes until lightly browned. Leave to cool, then store in a cookie jar for up to 1 month.

mixed spiced nuts

—very addictive

These very addictive nuts are just what you need in between meals or when you are feeling peckish. I love nuts, especially when they are spiced. You should be able to get Sriracha sauce from any larger supermarket or Asian supermarket.

1 can chickpeas, drained and rinsed
150g whole almonds
100g whole cashews
15g chia seeds
125g Sriracha chilli sauce
50g honey (or maple syrup, agave nectar
   or rice malt syrup)

1. Preheat the oven to 160°C / 140°C Fan / Gas Mark 2. Line a large rectangular baking tray with greaseproof paper.
2. Rinse the chickpeas thoroughly. Drain and pat dry with a kitchen towel. Transfer to the mixing bowl along with the whole almonds, whole cashews, chia seeds, Sriracha chilli sauce and honey then combine **10 Sec. / Reverse / Speed 2.**
3. Pour the nuts onto the prepared baking tray and spread out evenly. Roast for 30 minutes, stirring every 10 minutes, until a deep golden brown.

chocolate cookie sandwiches

There is not much to say here because the picture speaks for itself! These chocolate cookie sandwiches are made with my famous notella (recipe originally published in *Practice Mix Perfect*). These cookies are the perfect healthy treat in between meals when you are craving that naughty chocolate bar. You can store the leftover notella in the fridge for up to 2 weeks and the cookies can be stored in a tin for up to 2 weeks as well.

150g hazelnuts	160g buckwheat flour
6 dates, pitted	75g hazelnuts, ground
40g cocoa powder	1 pinch sea salt flakes
200g maple syrup	125g maple syrup
120g almond milk	80g olive oil
1 Tbsp vanilla extract	

1. Preheat the oven to 200°C / 180°C Fan / Gas Mark 6.
2. Place the hazelnuts on a large rectangular tray lined with greaseproof paper and roast for 10 minutes. Leave to cool, then tip into the mixing bowl.
3. Add the dates, cocoa powder, maple syrup, almond milk and vanilla extract. Blitz **1 Min. 30 Sec. / Speed 10**. Transfer to a sterilised jar and set aside.
4. Line a large rectangular baking tray with greaseproof paper. Turn down the oven to 180°C / 160°C Fan / Gas Mark 4.
5. To make the cookies, place the buckwheat flour, ground hazelnuts, sea salt flakes, maple syrup and olive oil in the mixing bowl. Blitz **20 Sec. / Speed 6**. Take teaspoonfuls of the mixture and roll into balls using your hands. Place on the prepared tray, press down slightly then bake in the oven for 10-15 minutes until lightly golden. Transfer onto a wire rack and leave to cool.
6. Fill some of the notella mixture into a large piping bag and cut off the bottom 4cm. Pipe a dollop onto half the cookies and sandwich with the other half. Store in a cookie tin for up to 2 weeks.

oaty cookies

—they make a lovely pie crust as well

It's 3pm and you are sitting at your desk waiting for that chocolate bar to appear next to you. I have an idea, why don't you just whip up a batch of oaty cookies the evening before work and take them as snacks in your packed lunch? They are made with delicious ingredients, totally gluten free and vegan. The best thing is, they only take 10 seconds to prepare. These little yummy treats make a perfect lunchbox snack for the kids, too.

80g gluten free oats + extra for sprinkling
1 tsp gluten free baking powder
1 pinch sea salt flakes
30g soft coconut oil
40g maple syrup (or agave nectar
  or rice malt syrup)

1 tsp vanilla extract
1 ripe banana, halved
20g dried cranberries (or raisins)

1. Preheat the oven to 180°C / 160°C Fan / Gas Mark 4. Line a large rectangular baking tray with greaseproof paper.
2. Place the oats, baking powder, sea salt flakes, coconut oil, maple syrup, vanilla extract, banana and cranberries in the mixing bowl. Combine **20 Sec. / Reverse / Speed 4**.
3. Spoon tablespoonfuls of the mixture onto the tray, leaving plenty of space in between and flattening each cookie slightly with the back of a spoon. Sprinkle with some oats and bake in the oven for 15-20 minutes until golden brown. Store in a cookie jar for up to 2 weeks.

broccoli quinoa bites

—a versatile little snack

When you are craving a small snack and you don't fancy anything sweet, these little broccoli quinoa bites are just perfect because they are small, nutritious and fill you up quickly. It is almost like having a healthy pack of crisps with you. They make a great lunchbox snack for yourself or the kids and you can keep them in the fridge for up to 3 days. If you prefer them a little spicy, add a red chilli with the garlic and if you like it a little fresher and sharper, add a spring onion as well.

1 broccoli, cut into small florets
100g quinoa
1100g water
2 garlic cloves, peeled
½ lemon, juice and zest

25g spelt flour (wholegrain or plain)
1 pinch sea salt flakes
1 pinch black pepper
10g olive oil

1. Place the broccoli in the Varoma. Place the quinoa in the simmering basket and add the water to the mixing bowl. Cook **20 Min. / Varoma / Speed 1**. Discard the cooking water and leave the quinoa and broccoli to cool.
2. Place the garlic cloves and lemon zest in the mixing bowl. Chop **2 Sec. / Speed 7**. Scrape down with spatula. Add the cooled broccoli and quinoa, lemon juice, spelt flour, sea salt flakes and black pepper then combine **20 Sec. / Reverse / Speed 3**.
3. Form the mixture into small patties and either fry in a frying pan with some olive oil until browned or for a healthier option, place on a baking tray lined with greaseproof paper. Preheat the oven to 200°C / 180°C Fan / Gas Mark 6 and once hot bake the quinoa bites for 15 minutes until lightly golden. Serve with a tzatziki dip or beetroot hummus.

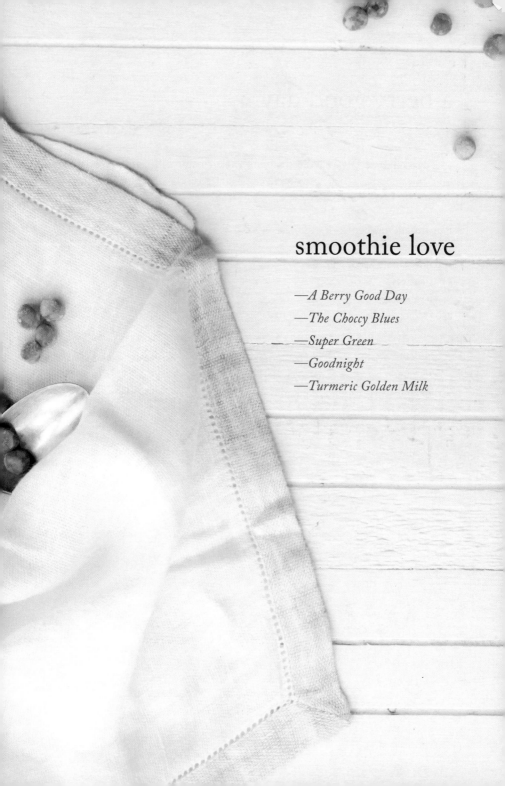

smoothie love

a berry good day

—strawberries, basil & pomegranate

Your day could not start any better than with a fresh smoothie that is packed with delicious fruit. This smoothie is so tasty; the strawberries and basil make the ultimate combination.

150g frozen strawberries
1 ripe banana, halved
½ pomegranate, seeds only
5 basil leaves
½ tsp vanilla extract
250g almond milk

1. Place the strawberries, bananas, pomegranate seeds, basil leaves, vanilla extract and almond milk in the mixing bowl. Blend 1 Min. / Speed 10.
2. Pour into two glasses and enjoy immediately or on your way to work. You can also make little to-go bottles for the kids.

the choccy blues

—blueberries, cocoa, avocado, nuts

I love everything about this smoothie. It is like a whole breakfast in a jar. So tasty and full of delicious ingredients. If you like it a little less sweet, you can leave out the maple syrup and if you don't like the nuts to be too overpowering, simply reduce the amount of nut butter.

2 ripe bananas, halved
½ avocado, stone removed
20g cocoa powder
100g nut butter of your choice
375g almond milk
40g maple syrup (optional)
50g blueberries

1. Place the bananas, avocado, cocoa powder, nut butter, almond milk and maple syrup in the mixing bowl. Blend **1 Min. / Speed 10**.
2. Pour the blueberries into the bottom of two glasses and smash them slightly with a fork. Pour the drink on top and enjoy immediately or on your way to work. You can also make little to-go bottles for the kids.

super green

—broccoli, peas & banana

This super green smoothie is a great way to get the kids to eat more veggies without them even knowing. Especially if you have some fussy ones who really don't like the look and taste of broccoli or peas – making them a smoothie is a great way to hide those 'ugly' looking veggie monsters. In this recipe I have used frozen vegetables, which is cost-efficient and still super fresh.

1 ripe banana, halved
50g frozen broccoli
50g frozen peas
5g linseed
10g fresh ginger
250g orange juice, with juicy bits
  (not from concentrate)

1. Place the banana, frozen broccoli, frozen peas, linseed, fresh ginger and orange juice in the mixing bowl. Blend **1 Min. / Speed 10**. Serve immediately or store in the fridge for up to 2 days. You can pour into small takeaway jugs for the kids to take to school or for yourself to take to the office.

goodnight

—calming, full of magnesium

Before you go to bed, it is time for one last drink. No, I am not referring to that glass of wine but this super tasty goodnight smoothie. It is made with calming ingredients and makes you feel happy and satisfied overnight. No more cravings at 1am.

1 ripe banana, halved
40g whole almonds
5g linseed
150g water
10g coconut oil
½ tsp vanilla extract

1. Place the banana, almonds, linseed, water, coconut oil and vanilla extract in the mixing bowl. Blend 1 Min. / Speed 10.
2. Pour into small glasses and serve half an hour before bed.

turmeric golden milk

—immune system booster

Turmeric is known to be a wonder spice. It is used in Asian cooking and has been praised by health experts for its anti-inflammatory powers. My mum drinks a glass of turmeric water every morning and when I presented her with the idea of turmeric golden milk, she was stunned. If you can get over the initial funny taste of turmeric and have a glass of this super colourful potion every morning, you might just develop the strongest immune system. When your colleagues are at home feeling sick, you will be the one sitting productively at your desk, laughing at the flu. You could even put some into your kids' morning smoothie.

75g whole almonds	20g manuka honey
75g whole cashews	½ tsp vanilla extract
30g fresh turmeric	1000g water
20g fresh ginger	1 pinch sea salt flakes

1. The evening before, soak the almonds and cashew nuts in a bowl with just enough water to cover the nuts.
2. In the morning, rinse the nuts and place in the mixing bowl along with the fresh turmeric, ginger, manuka honey, vanilla extract, water and sea salt flakes. Blend **1 Min. / Speed 10**.
3. Place a muslin cloth or a nut milk bag in the simmering basket. Pour the milk mixture over the cloth and strain into a bowl. Catch the milk and discard the leftover nuts. You can keep the golden milk in the fridge for up to 5 days. Have a glass of this milk every morning.

lush lunches & dinners

—Squash & Ginger Soup
—Cauliflower Pizza
—Baked Falafel Burgers
—Spiced Lamb Meatballs
—Gluten Free Pasta Dough

squash & ginger soup

—spicy and super creamy

One of my favourite flavour combinations is ginger and butternut squash. I love how this soup is both sweet and spicy and so incredibly creamy. If you prefer it less spicy, leave out the cayenne pepper – it does add a little kick to the soup. Any leftovers are perfect for office lunches and you can store them in preserving jars perfectly portioned up for lunch a couple of times a week.

½ large butternut squash, in 3cm cubes
30g fresh ginger, in 2cm slices
1 red onion, peeled and halved
2 garlic cloves, peeled
30g olive oil
1 can light coconut milk
500g water (if you prefer thick soups, only use 300g)

2 vegetable stock cubes (or 2 Tbsp homemade veggie stock paste)
½ tsp ground coriander
1 pinch cayenne pepper
½ tsp sea salt flakes
½ black pepper
1 tsp sweet paprika

1. Preheat the oven to 200°C / 180°C Fan / Gas Mark 6.
2. Line a large roasting tray with greaseproof paper. Place the butternut squash chunks on the tray and roast for 20 minutes.
3. Meanwhile, place the ginger, red onion and garlic cloves in the mixing bowl. Chop **2 Sec. / Speed 7**. Add the olive oil and fry **5 Min. / 120°C / Speed 1**.
4. Add the roasted squash, coconut milk, water, vegetable stock cubes, ground coriander, cayenne pepper, sea salt flakes, black pepper and paprika to the mixing bowl. Cook **15 Min. / 100°C / Speed Stir**.
5. Purée for 30 sec. starting on **Speed 4** and gradually going all the way up to **Speed 8**, ensuring the measuring cup is in place. Serve immediately. You can store the leftovers in the fridge for up to 3 days or take them in jars for lunch.

cauliflower pizza

—a gluten free 5-a-day dinner

If you are gluten free, then this is the pizza for you. It makes the perfect dinner and the cauliflower crust is so tasty. You can top it with anything you like and if you have fussy kids who don't like eating veg, this is a great way to disguise them in a tasty pizza.

750g cauliflower	1 garlic clove, peeled	1 aubergine
1000g water	1 can chopped tomatoes	1 red onion
100g ground almonds	10g tomato purée	100g mozzarella or feta
2 large eggs	½ tsp sea salt flakes	cheese
1 Tbsp dried oregano	1 pinch black pepper	10g fresh basil
	5g agave nectar (or maple syrup or rice malt syrup)	
	1 tsp dried oregano	

1. Preheat the oven to 200°C / 180°C Fan / Gas Mark 6.
2. Place half of the cauliflower in the mixing bowl. Blitz **2 Sec. / Speed 5**. Transfer into the Varoma lined with greaseproof paper. Repeat with the other half of the cauliflower.
3. Place the water in the mixing bowl. Place the Varoma on top. Steam **18 Min. / Varoma / Speed 1**. Remove and leave to cool slightly then rinse the mixing bowl.
4. Add the cooled cauliflower to the mixing bowl along with the ground almonds, eggs and dried oregano. Combine **15 Sec. / Reverse / Speed 3**. You might have to help a bit with your spatula until it is fully incorporated. Transfer the mixture onto either a large rectangular tray lined with greaseproof paper or two round pizza trays. Spread evenly and shape into a circle (or into a rectangle), making sure the edge is slightly thicker to build a 'crust'. Bake in the oven for 18 minutes.
5. Meanwhile, clean the mixing bowl and place the garlic clove in the cleaned bowl. Chop **2 Sec. / Speed 7**. Scrape down with spatula. Add the chopped tomatoes, tomato purée, sea salt flakes, black pepper, agave nectar and dried oregano. Combine **10 Sec. / Speed 6**. Pour into a small bowl and set aside.
6. Cut the aubergine into long, thin strips. Chop the onions into eight wedges and fry in a griddle pan for a couple of minutes until charred.
7. To assemble the pizza, remove the cauliflower crust from the oven, spread over the tomato sauce followed by the aubergines and onions and some cheese. Bake for another 15 minutes, then remove and sprinkle over the fresh basil. Serve immediately.

baked falafel burgers

—a lunch for the hungry ones

Sometimes at lunchtime you crave something a bit more substantial than just a salad. These super easy and delicious falafel burgers are just the right protein you need during the day. You can make them for the kids and use them as packed lunches for school or take them into work as a cold falafel burger. They also make great mini falafel balls.

25g fresh coriander	25g spelt flour (wholemeal or white)
2 garlic cloves, peeled	½ lemon, juice
2 spring onions	20g olive oil
1 can chickpeas, drained and rinsed	½ tsp sea salt flakes
1 tsp ground cumin	½ tsp black pepper
½ tsp smoked paprika	

1. Preheat the oven to 200°C / 180°C Fan / Gas Mark 6.
2. Line a large rectangular tray with greaseproof paper. Place the fresh coriander, garlic cloves and spring onions in the mixing bowl. Blitz **2 Sec. / Speed 7**. Scrape down with spatula. Add the chickpeas, cumin, smoked paprika, spelt flour, lemon juice, olive oil, sea salt flakes and black pepper then combine **10 Sec. / Speed 6**. If the mixture is still not sticking together, repeat for another 10 seconds.
3. Form the mixture into two large patties or four small patties using your hands. The mixture is sloppy but should be fairly easy to handle. Bake in the oven for 20-25 minutes for large patties or 15-20 minutes for smaller patties.
4. You can serve the burger patties hot or cold with wholemeal burger buns, slaw and a slice of tomato.

spiced lamb meatballs
—with fragrant spelt flatbreads

This has got to be my favourite lunch. I love lamb meatballs. Having said that, there was a time when I did not used to eat lamb as I didn't like the taste. But since I discovered these super tasty meatballs I have transformed into a lamb obsessed person. The spelt flatbreads go really well with them and combined with the spiced yoghurt make a perfect lunch. You can have them hot or cold and they are perfect for kids' lunchboxes.

200g spelt flour (wholemeal or plain) + extra for dusting 120g water 30g coconut oil ½ tsp sea salt flakes 400g Greek yoghurt ½ tsp ground cinnamon ½ tsp Kashmiri chilli powder	2 garlic cloves 10g fresh mint 10g fresh coriander 500g lamb mince 1 tsp garam masala ½ tsp Kashmiri chilli powder 1 tsp sea salt flakes 30g rapeseed oil

1. To make the flatbreads, place the spelt flour, water, coconut oil and sea salt flakes in the mixing bowl. Knead **1 Min. / Kneading Function**. Tip onto a lightly floured surface and divide into 4 equal pieces. Heat a large non-stick frying pan to medium heat. Roll one flatbread out to almost the size of the frying pan, approx. 18cm diameter and 3mm thickness. Fry the flatbread for about 45 seconds on each side until cooked and slightly browned. Wrap in a warm tea towel while you make the rest. Keep them wrapped in the tea towel while preparing the lamb meatballs. Clean the mixing bowl.
2. To make the spiced yoghurt, place the Greek yoghurt, ground cinnamon and Kashmiri chilli powder in the mixing bowl. Mix **10 Sec. / Speed 2.5**. Transfer to a small bowl and set aside. Clean the mixing bowl again.
3. Place the garlic cloves, fresh mint and fresh coriander in the mixing bowl. Blitz **1 Sec. / Turbo / 3-4x** until chopped finely. Scrape down using spatula. Add the lamb mince, garam masala, Kashmiri chilli powder and salt then combine **10 Sec. / Speed 6**. Form the mince into small balls using your hands and set onto a small plate.
4. Heat a non-stick frying pan with rapeseed oil and fry the meatballs for 10 minutes until golden brown and cooked through. Serve the yoghurt with the lamb and the flatbreads. You can make a small cucumber salad on the side to fill the flatbreads and wrap them up nicely.

gluten free pasta dough

Who said pasta can only be enjoyed with lots of gluten? Even without a pasta machine you can make this gluten free pasta dough in minutes. It is so elastic and once rolled out to your desired thickness you can make linguine, ravioli and more. Serve it with fresh tomato sauce and dry the rest of the pasta on a floured rack. If you wander around the house you will be surprised which spots look like a drying rack for pasta.

150g rice flour + extra for dusting
50g potato starch
25g cornflour
2 Tbsp psyllium husk powder
½ tsp sea salt flakes
3 large eggs
10g olive oil

1. Place the rice flour, potato starch, cornflour, psyllium husk powder, sea salt flakes, eggs and olive oil in the mixing bowl. Combine **20 Sec. / Speed 6**. The mixture will be crumbly.
2. Remove and transfer to a lightly floured surface. Shape into a ball and wrap in cling film. Leave to rest for 10 minutes, then uncover and cut in half. Make sure the other half of the dough is covered with a damp tea towel or stays wrapped in cling film.
3. Roll out one half of the dough into a long, thin rectangle about 3mm thick. It should be very easy to roll it out – if it sticks, just keep flouring the surface ever so slightly. Once rolled to the desired thickness, you can fold the rectangle and cut into linguine or cut out circles to make ravioli. You can use your pasta machine to make spaghetti as well. Or cut the rectangle into equal pieces and dry them to make lasagne sheets. Repeat with the other half of the dough. The dried pasta can be stored in a dry place for up to 4 weeks.

something sweet

—*Spiced Carrot Cake*
—*Guilt Free Key Lime Pie*
—*Very Choccy Ice Cream*
—*Healthy Lemon Tart*
—*Flourless Beetroot Chocolate Tart*

spiced carrot cake

—healthy twist on the popular teatime treat

Carrot cake always takes the centre spot at our afternoon tea table. Our family loves it and because everyone has recently started a diet, I have been experimenting with a version of the traditional cake that everyone can eat. The result is amazing. It is a spiced carrot cake with a beautiful height and fluffy texture. You can also add some yoghurt instead of buttercream, but it is not necessary.

150g carrots, in 4cm pieces
225g spelt flour (wholemeal or white)
1 Tbsp baking powder
1 pinch sea salt flakes
1 tsp ground cinnamon
¼ tsp ground nutmeg
120g apple purée (low sugar version
   or homemade)

55g Demerara sugar
½ orange, juice
100g almond milk
20g agave nectar (or maple syrup
   or rice malt syrup)
60g sunflower oil
50g walnuts

1. Preheat the oven to 180°C / 160°C Fan / Gas Mark 4. Line a 20cm round springform cake tin with greaseproof paper.
2. Place the carrots in the mixing bowl. Chop **4 Sec. / Speed 5**. Scrape down with spatula. Add the spelt flour, baking powder, sea salt flakes, ground cinnamon, ground nutmeg, apple purée, Demerara sugar, orange juice, almond milk, agave nectar, sunflower oil and walnuts. Combine **20 Sec. / Speed 5**. Pour the cake batter into the prepared cake tin and bake in the oven for 40 minutes until golden and a skewer inserted comes out clean. Leave to cool in the tin for 10 minutes, then transfer onto a wire rack to cool completely.

guilt free key lime pie

Key lime pie has been my favourite summer dessert for almost 20 years. I first tried it when I was about six and we went to the Florida Keys. It was so heavenly and I remember bringing a postcard home with the recipe for the original Florida Key lime pie. This super healthy version has very quickly become my best friend's favourite dessert and he took home half a cake after we had him over for dinner. I can't think of a better recipe tester than him. The best thing is, this pie stores well in the fridge for up to 1 week and makes a great packed lunch dessert because it contains virtually just fruit and veg. I even added my newest discovery to this recipe: vegan meringue. Go try that out, it is amazing!

80g gluten free oats +
   extra for sprinkling
1 tsp gluten free baking
   powder
1 pinch sea salt flakes
30g soft coconut oil
40g maple syrup
   (or agave nectar
   or rice malt syrup)
1 tsp vanilla extract
1 ripe banana, halved

3 firm but ripe avocados,
   stones removed
½ firm but ripe mango,
   stone removed
200g whole cashews
3 limes, zest
100g lime juice
100g agave nectar
   (or maple syrup
   or rice malt syrup)
200g coconut oil, soft

1 can chickpeas,
   liquid only (use the
   chickpeas to make
   a lovely hummus)
½ tsp cream of tartar
40g raw cane sugar
½ tsp vanilla extract

1. Preheat the oven to 180°C / 160°C Fan / Gas Mark 4. Line a 22cm loose bottom tart tin with greaseproof paper.
2. Place the oats, baking powder, sea salt flakes, coconut oil, maple syrup, vanilla extract and banana in the mixing bowl. Combine **20 Sec. / Reverse / Speed 4**. Spread the mixture over the base of the tart tin and bake for 15 minutes until golden brown. Leave to cool.
3. Clean the mixing bowl. Place the avocados, mango, cashews, lime zest and juice, agave nectar and coconut oil in the mixing bowl. Chop **10 Sec. / Speed 6**. Scrape down using spatula. Blend **1 Min. / Speed 10**. You might have to stop and pop the odd bubble that sometimes builds up—just keep an eye on it.
4. Spread the mixture over the cooled tart base and chill in the fridge for at least 2 hours.
5. To make the vegan meringue, insert the butterfly whisk. Add the chickpea liquid to the mixing bowl along with the cream of tartar. Mix **4 Min. / Speed 3.5**. Mix again **1 Min. / Speed 3.5** while adding the sugar and vanilla extract through hole in mixing bowl lid. Top the chilled pie with the meringue and serve.

very choccy ice cream
—a vegan dessert with only 4 ingredients

Can you believe a world where there is super tasty ice cream and it is not naughty? This chocolatey ice cream is one of the best inventions since brownies. Bananas are used to create a delicious flavour and the avocado adds some great, creamy texture. It makes a super healthy treat for the kids and you can omit the maple syrup if you like it less sweet. Just taste it when mixing and add sweetener if necessary. If you are looking for an extra fruity flavour, add some frozen raspberries as well.

3 bananas
½ ripe avocado, stone removed
40g cocoa powder
40g maple syrup

1. The evening before you want to make the ice cream, break up the bananas into small chunks (about 3cm) and place in a freezer bag. Freeze for at least 8 hours.
2. Place the bananas, avocado, cocoa powder and maple syrup in the mixing bowl. Blend **30 Sec. / Speed 6**. Scrape down using spatula. Insert the butterfly whisk and whisk **1 Min. / Speed 4**. Serve immediately or freeze until later. Take the ice cream out of the freezer 5 minutes before serving to allow it to soften slightly.

healthy lemon tart

Everybody loves lemon tart, or lemon bars or anything refreshing and citrusy in the summer. I have recently been on a mission to transform my super popular lemon bars recipe into a healthy version and have come up with this healthy lemon tart. It is the perfect dessert after a heavy meal and if you wish you can even make little lemon bars out of it by using a 20cm square tin instead. You don't even have to bake the almond crust but I find it adds a nice roasted flavour to the dessert.

200g whole almonds
60g desiccated coconut (unsweetened)
30g maple syrup (or agave nectar
   or rice malt syrup)

230g cashew nuts
200g boiling water
10g white chia seeds
145g maple syrup (or agave nectar
   or rice malt syrup)
3 lemons, zest
120g lemon juice
1 pinch ground turmeric (optional)
60g water
1 pinch sea salt flakes
180g coconut oil, soft

1. Preheat the oven to 180°C / 160°C Fan / Gas Mark 4.
2. Place the almonds, desiccated coconut and maple syrup in the mixing bowl. Crush **10 Sec. / Speed 10**. Pour into a 24cm tart tin and press down to create the shell. Bake in the oven for 5 minutes just until fragrant and roasted. Transfer into the fridge to harden and cool. Clean the mixing bowl.
3. Place the cashew nuts in a small bowl and pour over the boiling water. Leave to soften for 10 minutes, then pour off the water and tip the cashews into the mixing bowl.
4. Add the chia seeds, maple syrup, lemon zest and juice, ground turmeric, water, sea salt flakes and coconut oil then blend **1 Min. 30 Sec. / Speed 10**. Pour over the chilled tart base and chill in the fridge for at least 2 hours to set before serving. You can also freeze the tart if you prefer an extra refreshing dessert for the summer.

flourless beetroot chocolate tart

Sometimes it is not easy to find a good cake that is fluffy and also gluten free. This flourless beetroot chocolate tart is like heaven on a dessert plate. You can serve it slightly warm just after you've baked it or cold with Greek yoghurt. I would highly recommend adding some whole nuts and pouring the batter into a square tin to make brownies. You will be the most popular person at lunchtime, that is for sure. This cake does contain eggs but trust me, it is worth it.

125g dark chocolate (minimum 70%), in small chunks
300g cooked beetroot, peeled
4 large eggs
40g maple syrup
1 tsp vanilla extract

30g raw cocoa powder
1 Tbsp gluten free baking powder
1 pinch sea salt
125g ground almonds
40g olive oil

1. Preheat the oven to 180°C / 160°C Fan / Gas Mark 4. Line a 22cm loose bottom tart tin with greaseproof paper.
2. Place the dark chocolate in the mixing bowl. Chop **5 Sec. / Speed 7**. Scrape down using spatula, then melt **3 Min. / 37°C / Speed 2**. Transfer to a separate bowl and set aside.
3. Place the beetroot, eggs, maple syrup and vanilla extract in the mixing bowl. Combine **30 Sec. / Speed 5**. Scrape down using spatula. Then add the cocoa powder, baking powder, salt, ground almonds, olive oil and melted dark chocolate then combine **20 Sec. / Speed 4**.
4. Pour the mixture into the prepared tin and bake for 30-35 minutes until a skewer inserted comes out clean. Leave to cool in the tin for 10 minutes. You can also take it out slightly earlier and serve it as a gooey dessert. Can be served warm or cold.

Want more?

If you have got a taste for the delicious recipes I can offer for Thermomix, head over to my online shop at www.thermomixbakingblogger.com/shop where you will find my other books. All the accessories I have used in this book, such as nut milk bags, dough scrapers, bread proofing baskets, etc., can also be found in my shop.

First published in Great Britain in 2017 by Sophia Handschuh
Enquiries: admin@thermomixbakingblogger.com
www.thermomixbakingblogger.com

Text © Sophia Handschuh
Design © Sophia Handschuh and Jesse Sutton-Jones
Text design and typesetting by Anna Green at siulendesign.com
Photography © Sophia Handschuh